Honeysuckle

Mikayla Nadine Ross

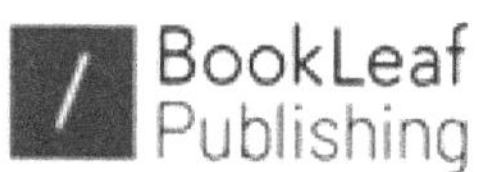

BookLeaf Publishing

Presentation by *BookLeaf Publishing*

Web: www.bookleafpub.com

E-mail: info@bookleafpub.com

ISBN: 9789357443616

First edition 2022

DEDICATION

This book is dedicated to those on a journey to heal-

Im right there with you.

ACKNOWLEDGEMENT

Thank you to the artist herself, Angelina Do.
Angelina Do is the artist of the cover of my first
book, Deep is Underrated and my second,
Honeysuckle.
And also - my Author's Image!
Angelina Do is an up and coming illustrator and
graphic designer.
Currently attending Canada's largest art and
design university; OCAD.

Check out her work! :
http://angelinatdo.myportfolio.com

Thank you, Angelina. I am so grateful for you
and your art.

PREFACE

Another collection of poetry,
another piece of my heart

beginning

she began,
then became.

too much

okay, listen,
I do not have the time,
for people who associate Mikayla with 'too
much'..
and for those who think I use an excuse for my
'attitude'
as a protective clutch
when I was younger, I get it but now?
constantly raising the tone
to prevent me from getting a word out
somehow?
I find it kind of funny that the ones who say all
this
are the ones that claim to love me
wouldn't they want me to utilize my talents
and bring in all the money?
I am not too loud, too emotional,
too much or too loving
they just don't know how to take it
God made me this way for a reason
and to suppress that is soul taking

kiss

marshmallows touch my lips
in passion
a soft but intricate interaction

heart speed increases
my knees they weaken
a touch sends goosebumps to rise

I try not to find
crimes in the lines
my tongue beneath another
they hide

an exchange bigger than we think
getting lost in lips meeting
causes thoughts to shrink

kisses feel like sunshine
on the stormiest night
the lights were once burnt out
but after a kiss now the home is bright

growing

I am growing,
it is showing,
by the shadow work I do

when its showing
I am knowing
the sun always comes back to you
when a person is upset
and I can feel that
I make space to feel it out

what I won't do is accept
when you give me all your doubt

I am a human just like you
please accept this truth
If not accepted, please forget it
I am the only one to approve

thank you, heartbreaks

thank you, heartbreakers
at first upon said break of heart
I wanted to name you numbered
but you did not get it wrong

Gods timing always delivers
in mysterious ways
it comes at a pace of life long song

all heartbreaks were different
none a carbon copy of another

I looked in the mirror every-time
and recited the line
"why can't they just love her?"

but I do she is my best-friend
I am my favorite person
and thank you for those,
heartbreaks
because I love every version

him

I've never felt something so passionate
is that how they explain it?
how do you get more?
I want it
my feelings aren't complacent.

you crave a human and a bond
when clock ticks, ties increase in strong

you are wrong
if you think spending time
will yield in your emotional side

or when they didn't listen,
Now all of a sudden they abide

am I fried?
or is finding yourself
beside someone else
the deepest wonder

and the peace you find with that other
induces the deepest slumber

or if you "what if"
before it happens
and now you can't recover

I'm starting to know a love so deep
I'm digging to discover

I hope that when he thinks of me
his thought is that
"I love her"
and deep down in our hearts we know

we're made up of each other

home

you are not a house,
you're a home

as long as i'm in your arms
I am never alone

found

I love being alone,
I've fallen in love with the sound

I am okay,
even when you're not around
If you wanted to see me,
you know that I'd be down

because you know that for loving you,
I would go the furthest bound

my love,
I hope I convey this message
even through the toughest ground

and I hope you know
that past me says
she is happy
I am found

breathing

I found illuminating life in my heart
when I thought breathlessness meant dying,
but I knew it was just the start

he

he was the force that moved me,
I didn't have a choice

and when he taught me speaking,
it was there I found my voice

I was once suffocated,
I didn't speak in fear

now, even under water,
you provide me breathing gear

you didn't stunt my growth,
in fact you played a part

I will always keep you safe,
because you protect my heart

misunderstood

I don't know why no one listens to me
but yet I am "too loud",
you say you want to applaud me,
yet you're not in the crowd

I am frustrated that I am always talked over,
I am choosing to move forward,
before my heart turns colder

I am older
than I used to be

that will continue to change
and while I continue to change
my heart will rearrange

I do not crave to be listened to,
because I give it to God
even though it hurts sometimes,
I would rather be a-lot

I have so many layers to peel back,

there is so much within my heart
I have so much to say
and so much in my way
so I will not stop this art

the more the merrier they say, don't they?
isn't that the truth?
the more they know is the more they say
i'm okay with being abstruse

smell

a smell can bring you back to June 2017
all of a sudden
your head is clear
and your room is clean

a certain candle creates flashbacks in your head,
then you wish you burned incense instead

a piece of clothing
can rewrite a scene
in your book
all of a sudden
the memory
becomes the hook
to say the least

when your thoughts they don't move
but your heart fastly beats

a smell can bring you back to 2004
when you didn't plan on moving
but all your stuff is at the door

a smell is a gift that lasts forever,
when your fingers have nothing to touch
and your eyes don't remember
the smell brings us back together

hello, my name is happy

hello, my name is happy
and I am here to stay

I just bought the place upstairs,
all hemispheres in disarray

I know who lived here before,
mr. sad and mr. down

I will dust the window panes
so healing will surround

I am a hard choice to make
I'm not always comfortable

I know what I need to do to get what I want
I need to be deemed vulnerable

happy chooses to be happy,
when even sadness is around

and happy will be there to cheer you up

when you feel down

happy is an everlasting choice
I cannot be somewhere else

happy is where I want to be
- heaven bound
I will never find my heart,
in hell

its okay

I never 'got over it'
I just moved on

I never found a melody
I wrote a new song

It's hard to find happy where sadness lives,
but the secret to that is finding space to forgive

people are seasonal sometimes
pre-written surprise contract

when the time is up sometimes
they add on tax

that's okay,
because if anyone leaves
I get to stay

it sucks sometimes I know,
but if you don't uproot the dead,
how will new flowers grow?

sundays

legend says
it took seven days
to create the universe

from the first to sixth day
the creator made
until there was
and on the seventh day
there was rest

which would have been a sunday
spending time, losing time together

throughout the day,
throughout the rain,
needless to say, you're on my brain

loud, cheerful music, home cooked food
resting, with my best friend
blankets, movies
before work tomorrow and I'm comfortable

you feel like these things
I especially am thankful on sundays,
for sundays

especially because
you can make any day
feel like a sunday

and sundays
remind me of you

six zero seven am

before the sun rises
I have flashbacks about our shut eyelids
and how waking up to you
feels like beautiful sun shining
even on overcast days

thinking about being in bed with you
makes me want to be your muse
I don't want to be your emotional disaster
I don't even have to be a sexual actor
I can just give you all of me with nothing in
between

conversing with you
I could do all the time
get lost in your mind
blinded by your shine
if you really want to know
what I'm thinking
you should've been mine
a hell of a far back time

and with the way I'm loitering
I'm about to get a fine

because looking into your eyes,
I'm sorry but addicting
this is getting interesting
when I'm inching closer to your face
listening to all the words in my way
hoping you have no objections in place

you are the judge, and I'm pleading this case

like a witness on the stand,
I'm not begging for innocence
I pleaded guilty willingly
and you are not silenced
however, if you are the judge,
and the case is between me and you,
the sun shining outside,
when we have things to do
just give me your word
and I promise you'll see
the bed I sleep in,
doesn't only have space for me

but a place for two,
when you happen to come by,
just for twenty minutes,
or until the sun shines

I was pretending to be blind,
but now the fog is clear,

I see

just like I've always wanted to be with
somebody,
now I want someone to be with me

rnb

they tell me,
your life is not an rnb song
the CD sticks
when it plays

all the blues others possess
does not stand in my way

my love I want it to be loud and stay
I want the truth to be portrayed

I wrote about the love I want
the powerful bond
I don't want it to be weak,
I want it to be strong

people who don't like love are boring
and people who give love are adoring
and the people who receive love are soaring
I want love like an rnb song,
never to skip a beat
I want to fill all the holes,
always be complete

and always spread love
to everyone I meet

concrete

"I am made for love", I said
'darling, what do you mean?'
"I told you I know the secret, to the birds and all
their bee's"

and I love that feeling you get, weak all in your
knees
and when the other wants to leave
I say
- no, stay, please

I was made for battles
I am tougher than I know
and I was made to teach
Im smarter than I show

I always tell the story,
of how from concrete flowers grow
a fertilizer found within,
impossible they claim, noh?

be strong always

one day in my life
I must have stumbled upon a problem,
and I had to choose strong or weak

that day I made a promise,
solemn,
that I would not accept defeat

I thought about the outcome
and who I'd like to be
I promised myself,
I'd never stray far from me

I came up with a phrase,
three simple words,
that I would never let out of my head

years later I'm happy,
doing this gladly,
reading them to remember instead

I stumbled upon it
and acknowledged

this has to be delivered in all ways
I find it fitting and quiet mind shifting
that young me pre-gave "be strong always"